This

The Li
Joke...ook

belongs to

_____

THE

LIGHTS OUT

JOKE BOOK

Katie Wales

Illustrated by Jean Baylis

RED FOX

A Red Fox Book

Published by Random Century Children's Books
20 Vauxhall Bridge Road, London SW1V 2SA

A division of the Random Century Group
London Melbourne Sydney Auckland
Johannesburg and agencies throughout the world

First published by Red Fox 1991

Text © Katie Wales 1991
Illustrations © Jean Baylis 1991

The right of Katie Wales and Jean Baylis to be
identified as the author and illustrator of this
work respectively has been asserted by them, in
accordance with the Copyright, Designs and
Patents Act, 1988.

Set in Century Schoolbook
Typeset by JH Graphics Ltd, Reading

Printed and bound in Great Britain by
Cox & Wyman Ltd, Reading

ISBN 0 09 973530 X

"Lights out, Tim!"

Contents

Facts For Insomniacs:

Can't get to sleep? Nod off with these. . .

★ You will turn over in bed between 60 and 70 times a night!

★ One third of Britain wakes up in the middle of the night

★ People who snore 4 to 6 nights a week have most car accidents!

★ People in Jersey sleep more than people in Scotland

★ There is actually a European Sleep Society! And a Sleep Research laboratory at Loughborough University

★ The average Briton wakes up at 7.01 a.m. One in 33 people is still asleep at 9.45 a.m.!

★ Most Britons are in bed by 11 p.m. The Scots and Irish are the last to bed; Midlanders the earliest

★ You spend about 23 years of your life asleep!

★ Women need less sleep than men

★ Mrs Thatcher needed just 5 hours of sleep a night. Sir Winston Churchill didn't need much sleep either. Albert Einstein spent 10 hours a night in bed! And the philosopher Schopenhaure liked at least 12 hours of sleep a night to help him think!

★ Most geniuses like to catnap: the average snooze lasts an hour

★ People who say they 'haven't slept a wink' have actually slept 40 winks!

★ Most people sleep between 7 and 9 hours a night

★ One man sleep-walked 100 miles by freight train, from Illinois to Indiana!

★ One British sleep-walker was charged with burglary, because he was found climbing a ladder at 3.30 a.m.!

★ Counting sheep does work if you can't get to sleep! Or reading *Lights Out* by Katie Wales .

★ A woman divorced her husband because he went to sleep on HER side of the bed!

★ Sleep-walkers CAN see, so they hardly ever bump into things. But they seldom know they've been sleep-walking

★ Ten per cent of all adults snore so loudly that they can be heard in the next room! Some people's snores are as loud as 80 decibels — the level of a fire alarm or a pneumatic drill!

★ One woman woke up to find that her sleep-walking butler had set a table for 14 people on her bed!

★ 30 per cent of all men and 19 per cent of all women snore every night; 50 per cent of all men snore occasionally, but only one third of all women do

★ People tend to snore more if they lie on their backs, are overweight, have a bad cold or tickly tonsils — or have false teeth!

★ One 'anti-snore' device is to sew a cotton reel or golf ball into the back of pyjamas!

★ The Americans have patented more than 300 anti-snore devices, such as chin-straps and electric shocks!

★ Prince Charles squirts toothpaste up his nose to stop himself snoring!

★ Some snorers are woken more than 300 times a night by their own snores!

★ Most people talk in their sleep

★ Rats sleep mostly in the daytime

★ Bats sleep 20 hours a day; a porcupine sleeps for 18 hours and mice for 13 hours. Moles sleep 8 hours; elephants sleep 3 to 4 hours and giraffes sleep for less than 10 minutes!

★ Bats really do sleep upside down!

★ Animals with hoofs (e.g. cows, horses, sheep) prefer to doze. So a cow sleeps for 4 hours, but dozes for 8 hours, eating at the same time! Cows and horses like to sleep standing up; but they only dream when they are lying down!

★ The right and left sides of a dolphin's brain sleep in turns!

★ The albatross and lark like to sleep while flying!

★ Cats and kangaroos like to sleep on their sides. Lions like to sleep on their backs. Leopards like to sleep on a branch with their legs dangling!

★ It's not easy to tell when pigeons, frogs and toads are asleep, because they keep their eyes open!

★ It's even more difficult to know when, or even *if*, ants sleep. They probably just have a rest period

★ Flamingos sleep standing on one leg, while sea-otters sleep on their backs in the water

★ There's a type of squirrel that hibernates for 9 months of the year

★ Dormice, like the one in *Alice in Wonderland*, really do sleep a lot: they spend most of their life snoozing and napping even when winter is over. The Romans thought fat little dormice were nice to eat!

★ You grow while you are asleep!

★ Your hair and nails grow more quickly at night than during the day!

★ It only takes you 15 minutes to get to sleep!

★ When you go to sleep, you drift first into a light sleep, then a deep sleep lasting for 30 minutes to an hour. You do this every night some four or five times

★ When you sleep, the only sense that doesn't switch off is your hearing (although we can sleep through alarm calls)!

★ Bedrooms are quite a 'modern' invention! In Europe, people used to sleep and eat all in one room, and put their visitors in their beds with them! Only royalty had bedrooms, and that's why kings held court there sometimes

★ In the Middle Ages people slept on straw. In Morocco people sleep on carpets

★ When animals like hamsters and dormice hibernate, their body temperatures fall close to freezing point

★ A baby spends two thirds of its time asleep in the first few days after birth.

★ Before school age, a child will spend on average 10 hours 18 minutes in bed!

★ Napoleon always went to bed between 10 p.m. and midnight and slept till 2.00 a.m. He worked till 5.00 a.m. and then went back to bed till 7.00 a.m.

★ One saint never slept for more than an hour and a half a day for 40 years!

★ A Californian man once spent 453 hours 40 minutes without sleep. That's nearly nineteen days

★ The word 'hypnosis' comes from the Greek god of sleep called Hypnos, son of the goddess of night

★ In the 15th century, a Belgian duke had a bed 5.79 metres long!

★ A Welsh vicar once spent 300 hours (12½ days) on a bed of nails!

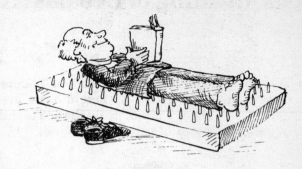

★ A bed to sleep 39 people was made in France in 1986

★ The largest blanket made in the USA took 13,000 hours to make: it measured 1100 square metres!

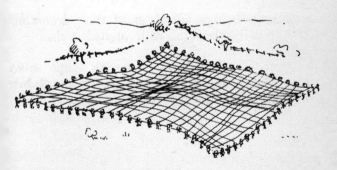

★ A chambermaid in a London hotel can expect to make more than 5000 beds a year . . .

The Meaning of Dreams...

★ Most people spend about one and a half hours dreaming every night. At first dreams are quite short: about 5 minutes. By the end of the night dreams can last up to 40 minutes!

★ Human beings spend more time dreaming than using their minds in anything else!

★ Some people believe dreaming helps solve problems. The first person to solve the Rubik Clock puzzle did it through a dream

★ Babies dream more than grown-ups; and many animals dream too

★ But no one really knows why we dream. Most dreams are about things that have happened to us during the day, all jumbled up. Perhaps dreams are meant to stop us getting bored in bed!

★ Fat people tend to dream more than thin people!

★ When you dream, your eyes are actually blinking very quickly

★ You remember very few of the dreams you actually dream. So even if you think you haven't been dreaming, you probably have!

★ Eating cheese and oysters is supposed to bring you nice dreams

★ You do dream in colour, but you forget the colours quickly when you wake up

★ Here are some things we might dream about that are supposed to be 'lucky':

apples; bananas; bald men; cocoa; marshmallows; milestones; mud; floating on water;

riding in a gondola; hailstorms; icicles; flying a
kite; climbing a ladder; eating oysters; running a race; pancakes; peacocks; pigeons; rain-
bows; roses; spiders; sheep; tortoises; trout;
turnips; umbrellas; violets; volcanos; zoos

★ Silly things can happen in dreams, but there's usually a 'story'. We dream mostly about ourselves, but we spend a lot of time talking and listening!

★ The Egyptians wrote about dreams in 2000 B.C. They thought that if a woman dreamt about a cat she would have lots of children! Many people have wondered about the 'meaning' of dreams, and written lots of books explaining them

★ People have been fascinated by dreams for thousands of years. The ancient Greeks thought people talked with the gods in dreams. Lots of myths and Bible stories give 'warnings' or 'commands' through dreams

★ People often have the same dream over and over again, perhaps because something is worrying them. These dreams can be about appearing in public with no clothes on! Or flying; or falling; or running but not moving; or missing the bus.

★ And here are some things we might dream about that are supposed to be 'unlucky':

bats; caterpillars; centipedes; chickens; writing for a magazine; moles; mustard; eating oranges; pearls; pigs; ravens; snails; shepherds; salad; salt; saucepans; sparrows; being thirsty; vegetables

★ You will receive a proposal of marriage or have success in love if you dream about:

cabbages; playing cards; cucumbers; earrings; geraniums; a glass of water; hornets; lilies of the valley; sewing-machines; mincepies; reading novels; pens; ponds; finding a purse; raspberries; rabbits; rhubarb; scissors; watching stars; wheelbarrows; Yorkshire pudding

★ But you will quarrel with your friends and sweethearts if you dream about:

beetroot; playing draughts; eyebrows; flies; forks; grass; hurricanes; kissing; eating leeks or lemons; fighting a lion; moving house; having two noses; otters; parrots; sinking ships; stomach ache; drinking tea; playing a trumpet; wriggling snakes; zebras

★ You will travel a lot if you dream about:

your head being back to front; lighthouses; limping; losing a ticket; salmon; walking on the beach; putting on a shirt; looking out of the window; witches; yawning!

Good Books to Read in Bed . . .

Time for Bed by I. M. Tired

So Tired by Carrie Mee

Lazy Bones by Eliza Sleep

Say Your Prayers by Neil Down

Baby Sitting by Justin Casey Howells

Hushabye Baby by Wendy Bough-Brakes

Don't Wake the Baby by Elsie Cries

Sleepless Nights by Eliza Wake

Noisy Nights by Constance Norah

What the Stars Mean by Horace Cope

Astronomy for Beginners by I. C. Stars

How to See Bats by Luke Sharp

Is There a Real Dracula? by Y. Knott

The Story of Dracula by Pearce Nex

A Guide to Transylvania by Bea Ware

Dracula's Victim by E. Drew Blud

How to Make your Own Monster by Frank N. Stein

Chased by a Werewolf by Claude Bottom

Ghosts and Ghoulies by Sue P. Natchrell

Witches and Warlocks by Eve L. Spirit

Vampires and Monsters by R. U. Scared

The Haunted House by Hugo First

Witch-Hunting for Beginners by Denise R. Nockin

Top Ten Spells by B. Witcher

Do UFOs Exist? by Athena Marshon

There is Life on Mars! by Bea Warned

Early One Morning by R. U. Upjohn

Reading Gravestones by Effie Taff

The Curse of Dracula by D. Ceased and B. Reeved

I Was Dracula's Prisoner by Terry Fied

Counting Sheep by I. C. Ewe

Jokes for Bed-Lovers . . .

What has four legs, but only one foot?
A bed.

Shall I tell you the joke about the bed?
I can't: it hasn't been made up yet!

Where do bed-lovers live?
Bedford.

How can you shorten a bed?
Don't sleep long on it.

Why did the bed spread?
Because it saw the pillow slip.

Why is breakfast in bed so easy?
It's just a few rolls and a turnover.

What's the laziest letter of the alphabet?
'E', because it's always in bed.

What question can never be answered with 'yes'?
'Are you asleep?'

What happened to Dozy who dreamed he was
eating a giant marshmallow?
*When he woke up, his pillow had gone! And he was
a little down in the mouth . . .*

Why did Dozy put his bed in the fireplace?
Because he wanted to sleep like a log.

Did you hear about Dozy who found a feather in his bed and thought he had chicken pox?

Did you hear about Dozy who slept with his head under the pillow? When he woke up, he discovered the fairies had taken all his teeth!

Why did Dozy climb on to the chandelier?
Because he was a light sleeper.

Why did Dozy take a tape measure to bed with him?
To see how long he slept.

Why did Dozy throw away his alarm clock?
It kept going off when he was asleep.

Why did Dozy take his bicycle to bed with him?
Because he didn't want to walk in his sleep.

Why didn't the banana snore?
It was afraid it would wake up the rest of the bunch.

Did you hear about Dozy who plugged his electric blanket into the toaster? He kept popping out of bed all night!

Did you hear about Dozy who put the TV to bed and watched the baby?

Did you hear about Dozy who slept under an old tractor? He wanted to wake up oily in the morning.

Did you hear about Dozy who heard a mouse squeaking one night, and got up to oil it?

Why did Dozy lose his job in the mattress factory?
He fell awake on the job.

Why did the gangster cut the legs off his bed?
He wanted to lie low for a while.

What did the cannibal say when he saw a sleeping missionary?
'Oh, yummy! Breakfast in bed!'

Why did the composer write music in bed?
He wrote sheet music.

Where do strawberries sleep?
In strawberry beds.

Why is a river lazy?
It never leaves its bed.

Why is the sea always restless?
It has so many rocks in its bed.

When is it proper to go to bed with your shoes on?
When you're a horse.

What horse sleeps only at night?
A nightmare.

Why did the jockey take hay to bed?
To feed his nightmares.

What should you do if you find an elephant asleep in your bed?
Sleep somewhere else!

How do you know if there's an elephant in your bed?
By the big E on his pyjamas.
How else?
There are peanut shells all over the bed.

How can you tell if there's an elephant under your bed?
When the bed touches the ceiling.

Do elephants snore?
Only when they're asleep.

What should you do it there's a tarantula in your bed?
Hide in the wardrobe!

What's the best advice to give a worm?
Sleep late!

What is a sleeping heifer called?
A bulldozer.

What's huge and grey and sends people to sleep?
A hypno-potamus.

What does a cat rest its head on when it goes to sleep?
A caterpillar.

'What side of the bed do you sleep on?'
DOZY: *'The top side!'*

DOZY: 'I'd like to buy a new bed, please.'
SHOP ASSISTANT: *'Certainly, sir. Spring mattress?'*
DOZY: 'Oh, no. I'd like to use it all the year round.'

BOSS: 'Why are you late for work?'
DOZY: *'There are eight of us in the family, but the alarm clock was set for seven.'*

DOZY: 'I want a divorce.'
JUDGE: *'Why?'*
DOZY: 'My wife smokes in bed.'
JUDGE: *'It's not that bad, is it?'*
DOZY: 'Yes it is. She smokes kippers!'

'Why do you comb your hair before going to bed?'
DOZY: *'To make a good impression on the pillow.'*

DOZY: 'My bed's too short and every night my feet freeze because they stick out from under the covers.'
'Why don't you curl up so you can put your feet under the covers?'
DOZY: 'What? I'm not putting those cold things in bed with me!'

'Doctor, doctor, I can't get to sleep at night.'
'Lie on the edge of the bed, then, and you'll soon drop off.'

'Doctor, doctor, how can I cure myself of sleep-walking?'
'Put drawing-pins on the bedroom floor.'

Doctor, doctor, I'm always dreaming about cricket.'
'Don't you ever dream about girls?'
'What? And miss my innings?'

'Doctor, doctor, I haven't slept for days.'
'Why not?'
'Because I sleep at night!'

'Doctor, doctor, I wake up feeling terrible! My head spins and the room goes round and round!'
'You must be sleeping like a top!'

'Doctor, doctor, I walk in my sleep!'
'Remember to take money for the bus, then!'

What did Sir Lancelot wear to bed?
A knight-gown.

What is the softest bed for a baby to sleep on?
Cot-on wool.

How do you get a baby astronaut to sleep?
Rock-et.

Where do baby monkeys sleep?
Apri-cots.

How do you know when someone is sleeping like a log?
When you hear them sawing.

What does one good turn do for you?
Give you all the blankets.

Did you hear about the parents who called their baby 'Caffeine' because it kept them awake all night?

What overpowers you without hurting you?
Sleep.

Why do people go to bed?
Because the bed won't go to them.

What's the difference between a feather bed and a poor man?
One is soft down, the other is hard up.

Jokes to Hibernate With . . .

What animal hibernates standing on its head?
Yoga Bear.

What's the best way to hunt bear?
With no clothes on.

What's white, furry and smells of peppermint?
A polo bear.

How can you tell where a bear lives?
Look for his Den mark.

Why does a bear have a fur coat?
He'd look silly in a plastic mac!

Why do dormice turn round and round before they go to sleep?
Because one good turn deserves another.

How do dormice kiss?
Mouse-to-mouse.

What is a dormouse's favourite game?
Hide 'n' squeak.

Where do hamsters go on holiday?
Hamsterdam.

What's small, furry and sleepy and likes corn?
A combine hamster.

What was the tortoise doing on the M1?
About 5 metres an hour.

Why did the tortoise beat the hare?
Nothing goes faster than Shell.

What are two hedgehogs called?
A prickly pair.

What do hedgehogs like for supper?
Prickled onions.

What's yellow and prickly?
A cowardy custard hedgehog.

What's green and prickly?
A seasick hedgehog.

What do hedgehogs say when they kiss?
'OUCH!'

Why did the hedgehog cross the road?
To see his flat mate.

Why else?
To pick up his squash partner.

What do you get if you cross a hedgehog with a skunk?
A smelly pincushion.

What do you get if you cross a hedgehog with a mole?
Leaky tunnels.

What do you get if you cross a hedgehog with a stinging nettle?
Very sore hands!

What do you get if you cross a hedgehog with a giraffe?
A 3-metre tall toothbrush.

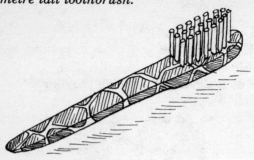

What's the best way to catch a squirrel?
Climb a tree and act like a nut.

What do squirrels give each other on Valentine's Day?
Forget-me-nuts.

What did the squirrel say to his girl-friend?
'I'm nuts about you.'

What animals use nutcrackers?
Toothless squirrels.

Where do squirrels go when they have a nervous breakdown?
To the nut-house.

What do you get if you cross a squirrel with a kangaroo?
An animal that keeps its nuts in its pockets.

What do you get if you cross a squirrel with an elephant?
An animal that remembers where it hid its nuts.

Jokes for Night Owls . . .

What is there more of the less you see?
Darkness.

What is the longest night of the year?
A fortnight.

Who's tall and dark and discos all night long?
Darth Raver.

What was Camelot famous for?
Its knight-life.

How did Noah see in the dark?
By ark-lights (or flood-lights!).

Did you hear about Dozy who drove his car into the lake one night?
He was trying to dip his headlights.

Did you hear about Dozy who sat up all night wondering where the sun had gone?
The next morning it dawned on him.

Why did Dozy have his sundial floodlit?
So he could tell the time at night.

Did you hear about the dozy night-owl who installed a skylight so he could watch the stars?
The people in the room above were furious . . .

What's big and bright and silly?
A fool moon.

What did the big star say to the little star?
'You're too young to go out at night.'

Where are starfish found?
In a planet-arium.

Which stars go to jail?
Shooting stars.

What did one shooting star say to the other?
'Pleased to meteor.'

Why are false teeth like stars?
They come out at night.

Two dozy drunks were staggering home one night.
One looked up and said: 'Is that the sun or the
moon?'
*'I don't know,' said the other. 'I don't live round here
either.'*

What makes the moon pale?
Atmos-fear.

What holds the moon up?
Moon beams.

When is the moon heaviest?
When it's full.

What fish swims only at night?
A starfish.

Why was the glow-worm sad?
Because it didn't know if it was coming or glowing.

How did the glow-worm feel when it backed into a tree?
De-lighted.

What makes a glow-worm glow?
It eats light meals.

What did one glow-worm say to the other when his light went out?
'Give me a push, my battery is dead.'

What do you get if you cross a glow-worm with a python?
A very long strip-light that can squeeze you to death.

What do call a clever glow-worm?
A bright spark.

Why is a cat longer at night than in the morning?
Because it's let out at night and taken in again in the morning.

'Mummy, mummy, should I put the cat out?'
'Why?'
'It's on fire!'

Where was the cat when the lights went out?
In the dark.

What game do cats play at night?
Trivial Purr-suit.

'You must take things quietly.'
I do, doctor, I'm a cat burglar!'

Did you hear about Dozy who thought he'd been burgled by a cat burglar? All that was taken was a pint of milk and a saucer . . .

Who wrote the *Thoughts of a China Cat*?
Chairman Miaow.

What do you get if you cross an alley cat with a canary?
A cheeping Tom.

What do cats read every night?
Evening mewspapers.

What else?
Moggyzines.

How does a cat cross the road?
By a purrdestrian crossing.

What do cats eat at night?
Mice Crispies.

What cat sleeps in the library?
A catalogue.

What noise does a cat make on the M1?
Miaaaaaooooow!

Did you hear about the cat who took first prize at
the bird show?
He ate the winning canary!

What's hot and greasy and goes 'hoot, hoot'?
Kentucky Fried Owl.

Why are owls cleverer than chickens?
Have you ever eaten Kentucky Fried Owl?

Why does an owl make everyone laugh?
Because it's such a hoot.

What would you get if you crossed an owl with a goat?
A hootenanny.

What would you get if you crossed an owl with a skunk?
A bird that smells, but doesn't give a hoot.

What sits on a tree and cries 'Hoots mon'?
A Scottish owl.

Why did the owl 'owl?
Because the woodpecker woodpecker.

What do lovesick owls say to each other when it's raining?
'To-wet-to-woo!'

What do you call a clever owl?
Bird Brain of Britain.

What book tells you about famous owls?
Who's Whoooo.

What's the difference between a wolf and a flea?
One howls on the prairie, the other prowls on the hairy.

What animal has wooden legs?
A timber wolf.

Why are wolves like cards?
They come in packs.

What do you get if you cross a wolf with a cockerel?
An animal that howls when the sun rises.

Did you hear about the wolves all-night party? It was a howling success!

Where do American wolves live?
Hairizona.

What did Mrs Wolf say to Mr Wolf?
'The baby's howling again.'

What kind of car do wolves drive?
A Wolfswagen.

What do bats do at night?
Aerobatics.

What did one bat say to another?
'Let's hang around.'

What would you get if you crossed a bat with a magician?
A flying sorcerer.

Spooky Jokes to Keep You Awake . . .

What do you get if you cross a spook with a packet of crisps?
Snacks that go crunch in the night.

Why are spooks bad at telling lies?
Because you can see through them.

Did you hear about the dozy spook? It climbed *over* walls.

Why was the spook lonely?
Because he had no body to go out with.

What do you call twin spooks who ring doorbells?
Dead ringers.

What did one spook say to another?
'You don't stand the ghost of a chance with me.'

What else?
'Do you believe in people?'

What do spooks wear in the rain?
Boo-oots and ghoul-oshes.

What did the headless spook say when he woke up?
'Oh dear, I must have nodded off.'

What do you get if you cross a spook with a policeman?
An inspectre.

What does a worried spook look like?
Grave.

What game to do spooks like to play?
Haunt 'n' seek.

What happens to dead authors?
They become ghost writers.

What kind of street do spooks like to haunt?
A dead end.

Who is a spook's favourite comedian?
Spook Milligan.

What spook appears on the front of a magazine?
A cover ghoul.

What did one spook say to the other?
'I don't know about you, but I'm dead on my feet.'

Who serves spirits on an aeroplane?
The air ghostess.

How do spooks get to work at night?
By ghost train.

What would you find in a haunted cellar?
Whines and spirits.

How do spooks get through a locked door?
With a skeleton key.

What do you do if you meet a skeleton on a dark night?
Jump out of your skin!

What do you call a skeleton that's always sleeping?
Lazy bones.

What did the mother ghost say to the baby ghost?
'Spook when you're spoken to.'

What's a spook's doctor called?
A surgical spirit.

What sort of song would a spook sing?
A haunting melody.

What do short-sighted ghosts wear?
Spooktacles.

When do spooks haunt skyscrapers?
When they're in high spirits.

Where do ghost trains stop?
At a manifestation.

How do spooks like their eggs?
Terri-fried.

What do ghosts eat for supper?
Spooketti.

What do spooks see at the theatre?
A phantomime.

What else?
The Phantom of the Opera.

What film do spooks like least?
Ghostbusters.

How do spooks like to travel?
By British Scareways.

Why did the spook fly from Heathrow?
He was on a night fright.

How do you send a letter to a spook?
Send it to the ghost office.

Why do spooks like the rain?
It's always in sheets.

What jewels do spooks wear?
Tombstones.

Where do spooks send their sheets?
To the dry screamers.

How does a spook start a letter?
'Tomb it may concern.'

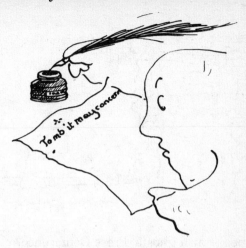

Why was the spook arrested?
Because it hadn't got a haunting licence.

What is a spooky boxer called?
A phantom-weight.

What do spooks like at fun-fairs?
The roller-ghoster.

What do you call a drunken spook?
A methylated spirit.

Where do spooks go swimming?
The Dead Sea.

How do spooks keep fit?
By exorcise.

Who speaks at a ghosts' Press Conference?
A spooksperson.

What does a spook guard say?
'Who ghost there?'

What does a spook read every day?
His horrorscope.

What trees do spooks like best?
Cemetrees.

What's a gargoyle?
What ghouls have for a sore throat.

What's a ghoul's favourite soup?
Scream of tomato.

What's a ghoul's favourite pudding?
Screeches and scream.

What do ghouls eat for breakfast?
Dreaded wheat.

What ghoul made friends with three bears?
Ghouldilocks.

What position do ghouls play in football?
Ghoulie.

Where do ghouls go on holiday?
Lake Eerie.

Where do ghouls like to haunt on Sundays?
Westmonster Abbey.

What did one zombie say to another?
'Will you be my ghoul-friend?'

What else?
'Beware my ghoulish heart.'

What else?
'You really kill me.'

Where do zombies study?
At ghoullege.

When is a zombie's holiday?
April Ghoul's Day.

What is a zombie lover's favourite song?
'If you were the only ghoul in the world.'

What did one demon say to another?
'Demons are a ghoul's best friend.'

What did the demon say about her companion?
'We're just good fiends.'

What is a demon's favourite drink?
Demonade.

What did one vampire say to another?
'I like your blood type.'

What else?
'I'm bats about you.'

Why don't vampires get kissed much?
They have bat breath.

What's a vampire's goodnight kiss?
Necking.

Who did the vampire marry?
The girl necks door.

Did you hear about the two vampires? They loved in vein . . .

What do you get if you cross a vampire with an elephant?
An animal that sucks your blood through its trunk.

Why are vampires mad?
Because they're bats.

Why are vampires unpopular?
Because they're a pain in the neck.

What dance do vampires like best?
The last vaults.

What do vampires eat with cheese?
Pickled organs.

What do vampires like for breakfast?
Ready Neck.

What's a vampire's favourite fruit?
A necktarine.

What else?
A blood orange.

Can a toothless vampire still bite you?
No, but it can give you a nasty suck!

Where does a vampire keep his money?
In a blood bank.

What do vampires do at midnight?
Take a coffin break.

What else?
Have a bite to eat.

What's pink, oinks, and drinks blood?
A hampire.

What has feathers, fangs, and goes 'Quack'?
Count Duckula.

What's Dracula's favourite song?
'Fangs for the Memory.'

Where does Dracula get his jokes from?
His crypt writer.

What's Dracula's favourite coffee?
De-coffin-ated.

Was Dracula ever married?
No, he was a bat*chelor.*

What do you get if you cross Dracula with Jack Frost?
Frostbite.

Where is Dracula's New York Office?
The top floor of the Vampire State Building.

What does Dracula take for a bad cold?
Coffin drops.

What did Dracula get on his birthday?
Lots of fangmail.

What do you get if you cross Dracula with a hot dog?
A fangfurter.

How can you join Dracula's fan club?
Send your name, address and blood group.

Why is Dracula's family so close?
Because blood is thicker than water.

What don't baby vampires believe in?
The tooth fairy.

What do you get if you cross Dracula with a midget?
A vampire that sucks blood from your toes.

Where does Dracula go for his holidays?
Gravesend.

Why did Dracula go to the doctor?
Because of the coffin.

What film did Dracula star in?
The Vampire Strikes Back.

What goes 'Chomp, suck, ouch?'
A vampire with a rotten fang.

What does Dracula have on his bath-towels?
'Hiss' and 'Hearse'.

What do you get if you cross Dracula with Saint George?
A bite in shining armour.

What did the dragon say when he saw Saint George in his shining armour?
'Oh no, not more tinned food!'

Why do dragons keep awake during the day?
So that they can fight knights.

What kind of planes do dragons like?
Spitfires.

What did one dragon say to the other?
'I wish I could give up smoking.'

What is a dragon's favourite flower?
The snapdragon.

What did one witch say to another?
'Hallo e'en.'

Where do witches go for their holidays?
Sandwitch.

What do witches eat for breakfast?
Snap, cackle and pop.

How do witches drink their tea?
With cups and sorcerers.

How does a witch travel without her broom?
She witch-hikes.

How does a witch tell the time?
With her witch-watch.

What do you call a nervous witch?
A twitch.

What is a witch on her broomstick called?
A flying sorcerer.

Why does a witch use a broomstick?
She'd look funny on a vacuum cleaner!

Why was the witch unhappy?
She couldn't spell properly.

What do you get if you cross a witch with an iceberg?
Cold spells.

What chocolates do witches like best?
Black Magic.

What name do you give a witch?
Witch Hazel.

'Mummy, mummy, what's a werewolf?'
'Be quiet, and comb your face.'

What do werewolves write on greetings cards?
'Best vicious.'

What did Mrs Werewolf say to Mr Werewolf, when he came home drunk?
'You're going to the dogs.'

Counting Sheep . . .

1 How do sheep get to sleep?
By counting people.

2 Why didn't the dozy farmer know how many sheep he had?
Whenever he tried to count them, he fell asleep!

3 Did you hear about Dozy who took up sheep farming, and failed because he planted them too close together?

4 'Doctor, doctor, I've just swallowed a sheep!'
'How do you feel?'
'Very baad!'

5 'Doctor, doctor, I can't sleep a wink.'
'Have you tried counting sheep?'
'Yes, I counted 842,511 – and then it was time to get up!'

6 Did you hear about the accountant who counted sheep in bed? He made a mistake in the first hour, and lay awake all night trying to figure it out!

7 Where do sheep get their fleece cut?
At the baaber's.

8 What keeps sheep warm at night?
Central bleating.

9 Why was the sheep arrested on the M1?
Because it did a ewe-turn.

10 Why do sheep like pubs?
Because they're full of baas.

11 Why don't sheep have much money?
Because they're always getting fleeced.

12 Where do Northern sheep come from?
Baarnard Castle.

13 Where do Southern sheep come from?
Ewell.

14 Where do London sheep live?
Lambeth.

15 Where do sheep go for their holidays?
Ramsgate.

16 Where do sheep go for their holidays abroad?
Baali.

17 Where do sheep go for their holidays in winter?
The Baahaamaas.

18 Where do sheep shop?
Woolworth's.

19 What do sheep find there?
Baagains.

20 Who is the sheep's favourite singer?
Baabara Streisand.

21 What is the sheep's favourite pop group?
The Pet Sheep Boys.

22 What is the sheep's favourite musician?
Chris Baaber.

23 What do sheep like to listen to at discos?
Ewe 2 and Ewe B 40.

24 What is the sheep's favourite song?
'I've got plenty of mutton.'

25 What do you call a sheep in the rain?
A wet blanket.

26 What side of a sheep has the most wool?
The outside.

27 If dogs have fleas, what do sheep have?
Fleece.

28 What did one sheep say to the other?
'I love ewe.'

29 What do sheep wear for work?
Ewe-niforms.

30 Why did the sheep stay quiet all day?
He didn't believe in bleating between meals.

31 What do you get if you cross a sheep with a kangaroo?
A woolly jumper.

32 What else?
A jumper with pockets.

33 What do you get if you cross a sheep with a gnu?
A new ewe.

34 What do you get if you cross a lamb with a penguin?
A sheepskin dinner jacket.

35 What do you get if you cross a sheep with an octopus?
A sweater with eight sleeves!

36 What do you get if you cross a sheep with an elephant?
Enough wool to knit a skyscraper.

37 What do you get if you cross a sheep with a hedgehog?
An animal that knits its own sweaters.

38 What do you get if you cross a sheep with a goat and a cow?
The Milky Baa Kid.

39 What do you get if you cross a sheep with a banana?
A baanaanaa.

40 Where are newborn lambs kept?
In an inc-ewe-bator.

41 What has fleece and fangs?
Drac-ewe-la.

42 What else?
A rampire.

43 What sheep is strong enough to hold up the world?
Herc-ewe-les.

44 What has fleece and big muscles?
Rambo.

45 What lives under water and bleats at ships?
A ewe-boat.

46 What do you call a sheep who tells sheep jokes?
A ewe-morist.

Other great reads *from* **Red Fox**

Further Red Fox titles that you might enjoy reading are listed on the following pages. They are available in bookshops or they can be ordered directly from us.

If you would like to order books, please send this form and the money due to:

ARROW BOOKS, BOOKSERVICE BY POST, PO BOX 29, DOUGLAS, ISLE OF MAN, BRITISH ISLES. Please enclose a cheque or postal order made out to Arrow Books Ltd for the amount due, plus 22p per book for postage and packing, both for orders within the UK and for overseas orders.

NAME _____

ADDRESS _____

_____

Please print clearly.

Whilst every effort is made to keep prices low, it is sometimes necessary to increase cover prices at short notice. If you are ordering books by post, to save delay it is advisable to phone to confirm the correct price. The number to ring is THE SALES DEPARTMENT 071 (if outside London) 973 9700.

Other great reads ✎ *from* **Red Fox**

The latest and funniest joke books are from Red Fox!

THE OZONE FRIENDLY JOKE BOOK
Kim Harris, Chris Langham, Robert Lee,
Richard Turner

What's green and highly dangerous?
How do you start a row between conservationists?
What's green and can't be rubbed out?

Green jokes for green people (non-greens will be pea-green when they see how hard you're laughing), bags and bags of them (biodegradable of course).

All the jokes in this book are printed on environmentally friendly paper and every copy you buy will help GREENPEACE save our planet.

* David Bellamy with a machine gun.
* Pour oil on troubled waters.
* The Indelible hulk.

ISBN 0 09 973190 8   £1.99

THE HAUNTED HOUSE JOKE BOOK
John Hegarty

There are skeletons in the scullery . . .
Beasties in the bath . . .
There are spooks in the sitting room
And jokes to make you laugh . . .

Search your home and see if we are right. Then come back, sit down and shudder to the hauntingly funny and eerily rib-rattling jokes in this book.

ISBN 0 09 9621509   £1.99

Other great reads from **Red Fox**

AMAZING ORIGAMI FOR CHILDREN
Steve and Megumi Biddle

Origami is an exciting and easy way to make toys, decorations and all kinds of useful things from folded paper.

Use leftover gift paper to make a party hat and a fancy box. Or create a colourful lorry, a pretty rose and a zoo full of origami animals. There are over 50 fun projects in Amazing Origami.

Following Steve and Megumi's step-by-step instructions and clear drawings, you'll amaze your friends and family with your magical paper creations.

ISBN 0 09 9661802   £4.99

MAGICAL STRING   Steve and Megumi Biddle

With only a loop of string you can make all kinds of shapes, puzzles and games. Steve and Megumi Biddle provide all the instructions and diagrams that are needed to create their amazing string magic in another of their inventive and absorbing books.

ISBN 0 09 964470 3   £2.50

Other great reads from **Red Fox**

Discover the exciting and hilarious books of Hazel Townson!

THE MOVING STATUE

One windy day in the middle of his paper round, Jason Riddle is blown against the town's war memorial statue.

But the statue moves its foot! Can this be true?

ISBN 0 09 973370 6 £1.99

ONE GREEN BOTTLE

Tim Evans has invented a fantasic new board game called REDUNDO. But after he leaves it at his local toy shop it disappears! Could Mr Snyder, the wily toy shop owner have stolen the game to develop it for himself? Tim and his friend Doggo decide to take drastic action and with the help of a mysterious green bottle, plan a Reign of Terror.

ISBN 0 09 956810 1 £1.50

THE SPECKLED PANIC

When Kip buys Venger's Speckled Truthpaste instead of toothpaste, funny things start happening. But they get out of control when the headmaster eats some by mistake. What terrible truths will he tell the parents on speech day?

ISBN 0 09 935490 X £1.75

THE CHOKING PERIL

In this sequel to *The Speckled Panic*, Herbie, Kip and Arthur Venger the inventor attempt to reform Grumpton's litterbugs.

ISBN 0 09 950530 4 £1.25